DISCOVER
AMERICA

NORTH CAROLINA

Jill Foran

MEDIA ENHANCED BOOKS

AV²
BY WEIGL™

ADDED VALUE • AUDIO VISUAL

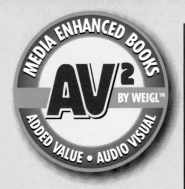

AV[2] provides enriched content that supplements and complements this book. Weigl's AV[2] books strive to create inspired learning and engage young minds in a total learning experience.

Your AV[2] Media Enhanced books come alive with...

Audio
Listen to sections of the book read aloud.

Key Words
Study vocabulary, and complete a matching word activity.

Video
Watch informative video clips.

Quizzes
Test your knowledge.

Embedded Weblinks
Gain additional information for research.

Slide Show
View images and captions, and prepare a presentation.

Try This!
Complete activities and hands-on experiments.

... and much, much more!

Go to **www.av2books.com**, and enter this book's unique code.

BOOK CODE

P 8 6 8 9 8 6

AV[2] by Weigl brings you media enhanced books that support active learning.

Published by AV[2] by Weigl
350 5th Avenue, 59th Floor
New York, NY 10118
Website: www.av2books.com

Library of Congress Cataloging-in-Publication Data
Names: Foran, Jill, author.
Title: North Carolina : the Tar Heel State / Jill Foran.
Description: New York, NY : AV2 by Weigl, [2016] | Series: Discover America |
  Includes index.
Identifiers: LCCN 2015048026 (print) | LCCN 2015048331 (ebook) | ISBN
  9781489649140 (hard cover : alk. paper) | ISBN 9781489649157 (soft cover :
  alk. paper) | ISBN 9781489649164 (Multi-User eBook)
Subjects: LCSH: North Carolina--Juvenile literature.
Classification: LCC F254.3 .F662 2016 (print) | LCC F254.3 (ebook) | DDC 975.6--dc23
LC record available at http://lccn.loc.gov/2015048026

Printed in the United States of America, in Brainerd, Minnesota
1 2 3 4 5 6 7 8 9 20 19 18 17 16

082016
210716

Project Coordinator Heather Kissock
Art Director Terry Paulhus

Photo Credits
Every reasonable effort has been made to trace ownership and to obtain permission to reprint copyright material. The publisher would be pleased to have any errors or omissions brought to their attention so that they may be corrected in subsequent printings. The publisher acknowledges Getty

NORTH CAROLINA

Contents

STATE TREE
Pine

STATE BIRD
Cardinal

STATE MAMMAL
Gray Squirrel

STATE FLAG
North Carolina

STATE FLOWER
Dogwood

STATE SEAL
North Carolina

The Tar Heel State

Esse Quam Videri
(To Be Rather Than to Seem)

"The Old North State," words
by William Gaston, sung to a
traditional melody arranged
by Mrs. E. E. Randolph

(2010 Census) 9,535,483
Ranked 10th state

November 21, 1789, as the 12th state

Raleigh

Discover North Carolina

North Carolina is located along the Atlantic coast, in the southeastern United States. To its west is Tennessee, to its north is Virginia, and to its south are South Carolina and Georgia. The state is closely tied to the first era of European colonization, due to its location on the eastern edge of North America. Its coastline is dotted with lighthouses, particularly along the Outer Banks, a chain of sandy islands along the coast. Situated on the easternmost point of North Carolina, Cape Hatteras has been the site of many shipwrecks.

North Carolina is known as the Tar Heel State. Historians disagree about the origin of the nickname. Some believe that it dates back to colonial days, when North Carolina was a leading producer of tar. Others trace the name to the Civil War. During one battle, North Carolina's soldiers refused to retreat, as if their heels were glued to the ground with tar.

There are many ways to get to North Carolina. The state has ports along the Intracoastal Waterway, which is a protected sailing route along the Atlantic coast. Several major interstate highways run through the state, and secondary highways provide access to the state's towns and cities. Rail service is also available, with Amtrak passenger trains offering daily trips across the state. North Carolina has several international and regional airports. The busiest airports are in Charlotte and Raleigh-Durham. The Charlotte Area Transit System, or CATS, opened its first light-rail line in 2007.

The Land

Biltmore Estate, built by George Washington Vanderbilt II in 1895, is the largest privately owned home in the United States.

North Carolina is divided into **100 counties.**

The largest state-maintained **highway system** in the U.S. belongs to North Carolina.

Orville Wright flew the first successful airplane flight at 10:35 am on December 17, 1903. He flew for 12 seconds and rose 120 feet into the air.

Beginnings

One of the original 13 states of the United States, North Carolina is rich with history. In 1587, it was the birthplace of the first child born of British parents in America. For many years, residents were unhappy with the rule of its distant British proprietors, and by 1768, North Carolinians had begun to defy British rule in more direct ways. They organized rebellions, eventually chasing the British governor out of the colony in 1775. The state was the second to declare independence from Great Britain, and became the twelfth state in the Union.

Slavery played a major role in North Carolina's farm economy during the state's early years. African American slaves planted and harvested most crops. By 1860, one of every three North Carolinians was an African American slave. North Carolina fought on the Confederate side during the Civil War. After the Union won the war in 1865, slavery was **abolished** across the United States. North Carolinians rebuilt the state quickly after the war. By the end of the 1800s, agriculture and other industries were once again prosperous.

In 1903, near Kitty Hawk, Wilbur and Orville Wright conducted the first successful airplane flight. The state has become known for its excellent research facilities and its highly respected colleges and universities. The University of North Carolina at Chapel Hill was founded in 1789. It is the oldest university in the state, and is also one of the oldest publicly-funded universities in the United States.

Where is
NORTH CAROLINA

North Carolina covers a total area of 53,819 square miles, of which land makes up about 90 percent and water 10 percent. The state's coastline is very irregular, with many bays, inlets, and islands. Including all these indentations, the shoreline measures 3,375 miles. The state is the 9th most populated state in the union and its two most populated cities are among the fastest-growing in the United States. North Carolina is divided into 100 counties.

TENNESSEE

United States Map

North Carolina

Alaska Hawai'i

MAP LEGEND

- North Carolina
- ☆ Capital City
- ● Major City
- ▲ Pocosin Lakes National Wildlife Refuge
- ■ Moores Creek
- □ Bordering States
- □ Water

SOUTH CAROLINA

1 Raleigh

North Carolina has had several state capitals. Raleigh became the capital in 1792, and the state legislature began meeting there two years later. Today, Raleigh and nearby Durham and Chapel Hill form a metropolitan region with more than 1.2 million people.

2 Pocosin Lakes National Wildlife Refuge

Just outside of Columbia, the Pocosin Lakes National Wildlife Refuge covers 110,000 acres. The refuge was established in 1990 to preserve the wetlands and native wildlife. It also serves as a home for migratory birds and endangered species such as the red wolf.

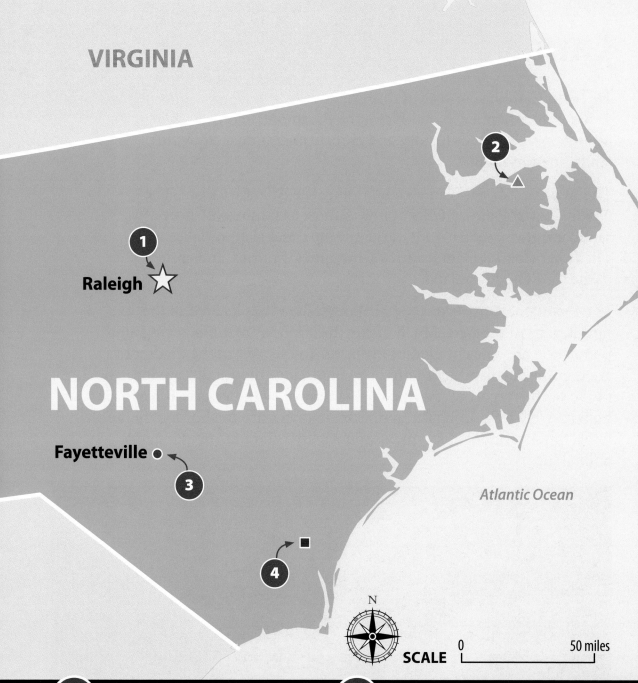

VIRGINIA

NORTH CAROLINA

1 Raleigh

Fayetteville ●

3

Atlantic Ocean

4 ■

2 ▲

N

SCALE

0   50 miles

---

3 **Fayetteville**

Fayetteville was the state capital from 1789 to 1793. Today, its economy is centered around Fort Bragg, to the north, and the Pope Air Force Base, to the northwest. In 2008, Fayetteville announced it would be a sanctuary city for soldiers and military families. They are provided with social services, job placement, and discounts at various stores.

4 **Moores Creek**

In February of 1776, the Battle of Moores Creek became the first Patriot victory in the American Revolutionary War. The Moores Creek National Battlefield was established in 1980 to commemorate this triumph. Today, visitors can experience a candlelight guided tour that recreates the sights and sounds of the battle.

Land Features

North Carolina consists of three natural land regions. These regions are the Atlantic Coastal Plain, the Piedmont, and the Appalachian Mountains. The state's history and climate are influenced by this landscape variation.

The Atlantic Coastal Plain extends along the Atlantic Ocean. The Outer Coastal Plain consists of low islands, hazardous offshore sandbars, grassy marshlands, large swamps, and shallow lakes. The Inner Coastal Plain features sand dunes, prairies, and some of the state's best farmland.

The Piedmont consists of gently rolling hills, and is located in the middle part of the state. Much of North Carolina's manufacturing and population are concentrated in this area. To the west of the Piedmont are the Appalachian Mountains. The Blue Ridge mountains are located in the southern part of the Appalachian range, with peaks that reach as high as 6,000 feet. Along the Tennessee-North Carolina border are the Great Smoky Mountains, which support large amounts of plant and animal life.

Whitewater Falls

Located about 60 miles from Asheville, Whitewater Falls is the highest waterfall east of the Mississippi River.

Great Dismal Swamp

Since 1974, portions of the Great Dismal Swamp have been designated as a national wildlife refuge.

Great Smoky Mountains

Great Smoky Mountains National Park is part of the Blue Ridge Mountains. The area is the most-visited National Park in the United States.

Outer Banks

The Outer Banks are sandy barrier islands that extend about 200 miles along North Carolina's Atlantic coast.

Climate

Average January temperatures in North Carolina range from 40° to 45° Fahrenheit in most areas. In summer, the average temperature for the state is 84°F, though the mountains can be up to 20° cooler. The highest temperature ever recorded in the state was 110°F in Fayetteville, in 1983. The record low temperature was –34°F on Mt. Mitchell, in 1985.

Average Annual Precipitation Across North Carolina

The average annual precipitation varies for different areas across North Carolina. How does location affect the amount of precipitation an area receives?

LEGEND

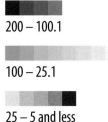

Average Annual Precipitation (in inches) 1961–1990

200 – 100.1

100 – 25.1

25 – 5 and less

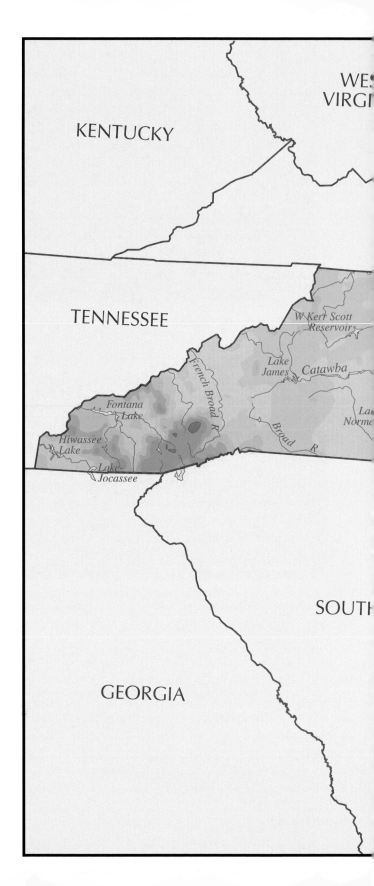

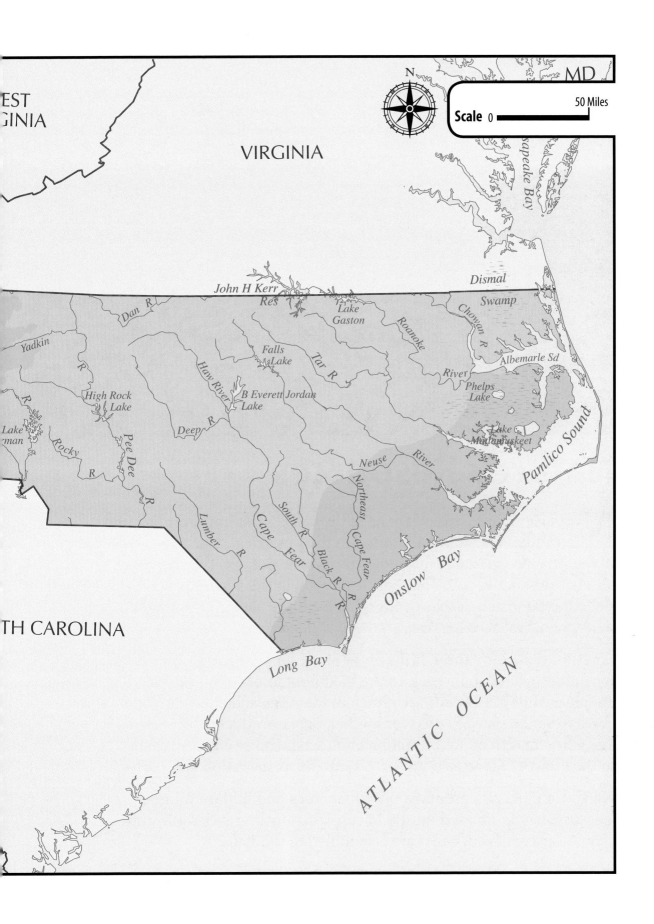

In 2014, tobacco production generated $453 million of revenue for North Carolina.

Nature's Resources

North Carolina's rich soil is one of the state's most important natural resources. The sandy soil found in the western and central parts of the Atlantic Coastal Plain is ideal for growing crops. The Piedmont also has productive soil. The most fertile soil in this region contains rich **alluvial** materials. North Carolina leads the nation in the value of its annual tobacco harvest.

Forests cover nearly three-fifths of the state, supplying raw materials for timber-related industries. In the Piedmont, most trees harvested are pine, while hardwoods are grown in the Appalachian Mountains. Trees from the state are used for lumber, paper products, furniture, and Christmas trees. Reforestation and sustainability efforts have led to the growth of forests in the state, both for conservation and harvest.

North Carolina also produces phosphate rock and lithium minerals. These materials are used mostly in construction as gravel, sand, and clay. A variety of gemstones are also mined in the state.

Many different types of quartz are mined in North Carolina. Some are ground down into quartz sand, which is used for industrial purposes.

In recent years, the forest products industry has become North Carolina's top manufacturing industry.

Vegetation

North Carolina's dense forests contain many kinds of trees. Pines are plentiful on the Atlantic Coastal Plain. Hardwoods such as oak, ash, and hickory grow in the mountains. The Piedmont has a mix of evergreens and hardwoods. White cedars, black tupelos, and sweet gums grow in swamps and along rivers. The Black River area contains bald cypress trees. Some are 1,700 years old, making them the oldest known trees in the country east of the Rocky Mountains.

The Atlantic Coastal Plain is recognized for its distinctive plant life. About a dozen **carnivorous** plants grow in the state's swampy areas. One of the most interesting of these is the Venus flytrap. This plant traps insects by closing its leaves over them, and then digesting them.

Flowering Dogwood

Standing up to 30 feet tall, the flowering dogwood prefers partial shade and moist, well-drained soil.

Bald Cypress

Bald cypress trees usually grow 50 to 100 feet tall and thrive in a wide variety of North Carolina soils.

Lily

The Stargazer lily reaches heights of 3 feet or more and usually blooms in midsummer.

Venus Flytrap

After closing over an insect, the leaves of the Venus flytrap can take up to two weeks to digest their prey.

Wildlife

North Carolina is home to a wide range of animals. Mammals include bears, wildcats, deer, raccoons, and opossums. Thousands of black bears live in the western mountains and in parts of the Atlantic Coastal Plain. The coastal plain also serves as habitat for many reptile species, including the American alligator, the largest reptile in North America. Several thousand alligators live in the state's southeastern swamps and rivers.

Birds common in North Carolina include the cardinal, wren, mockingbird, chickadee, woodpecker, and warbler. Wild turkeys, quails, and doves are also found in abundance. During winter months, many bald eagles can be seen in Uwharrie National Forest. The eagles are attracted to the easy fishing that the forest's **reservoirs** offer.

Among the many fish species found in the state's lakes and rivers are trout, bass, perch, bluegill, and crappies. The coastal waters are home to sea trout, sharks, Atlantic croakers, blue crabs, and shrimps. Rainbow and brook trout live in mountain streams.

Black Bear

The maximum weight ever recorded for a bear in North Carolina is 880 pounds.

Wild Turkey

Wildlife experts succeeded in boosting the state's wild turkey population from 2,000 in 1970 to 150,000 by 2005.

Cardinal

The cardinal became the state bird in 1943. Primarily a seed eater, it also feeds on small fruits and insects.

Eastern Box Turtle

Adapted to a wide variety of habitats, eastern box turtles in North Carolina are most often found in damp, forested areas with plenty of underbrush.

Economy

Whitewater Adventures

The rugged rivers of western North Carolina can challenge even the most experienced kayakers and canoeists.

Tourism

The Great Smoky Mountains National Park covers more than 800 square miles and stretches into Tennessee. Visitors can mountain bike, hike, and camp within the park's borders. Many vacationers also travel to the coast to enjoy the unspoiled beaches, quiet resort towns, and majestic lighthouses of the Outer Banks. One of North Carolina's most popular historic sites is the Wright Brothers National Memorial at Kitty Hawk. This memorial stands near the location of their first successful motor-powered flight.

Fort Raleigh

At the Fort Raleigh National Historic Site, **archaeologists** and historians continue to unravel the mystery of what happened to Great Britain's "Lost Colony" in the 1580s.

Cape Hatteras Lighthouse

More than 200 feet high, the Cape Hatteras Lighthouse overlooks Cape Hatteras National Seashore and the treacherous Diamond Shoals.

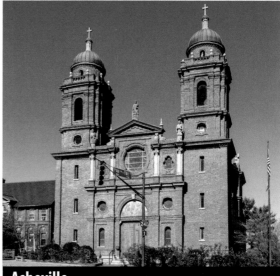

Asheville

Lush countryside, fine hotels, and top-quality cultural attractions make Asheville one of North Carolina's most popular resort regions.

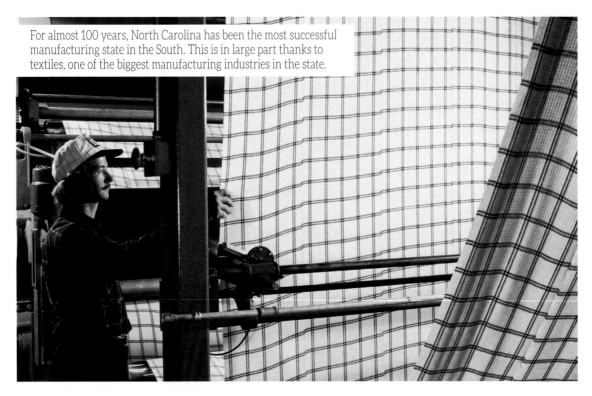

For almost 100 years, North Carolina has been the most successful manufacturing state in the South. This is in large part thanks to textiles, one of the biggest manufacturing industries in the state.

Primary Industries

North Carolina is among the country's leading industrial states. Long-established manufacturing industries include textiles, wooden furniture, and cigarettes. Among North Carolina's newer industries are industrial machinery and computers, electronic equipment, and chemicals. Many companies have established high-technology research facilities in an area called Research Triangle Park, located near Raleigh, Durham, and Chapel Hill.

Agriculture was formerly the leading industry in North Carolina. Today, agriculture, forestry, and fishing employ a relatively small share of the work force. The main crops include tobacco, sweet potatoes, cotton, soybeans, corn, and peanuts. Livestock farms raise pigs, poultry, and cattle.

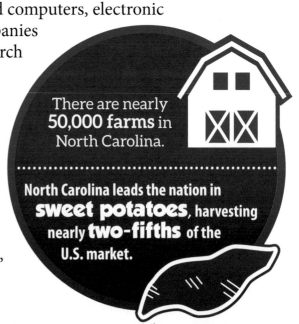

There are nearly **50,000 farms** in North Carolina.

North Carolina leads the nation in **sweet potatoes**, harvesting nearly **two-fifths** of the U.S. market.

Value of Goods and Services (in Millions of Dollars)

Finance, insurance, and real estate now makes up one of the largest segments of North Carolina's economy. What factors account for the rapid growth of this industry in recent decades?

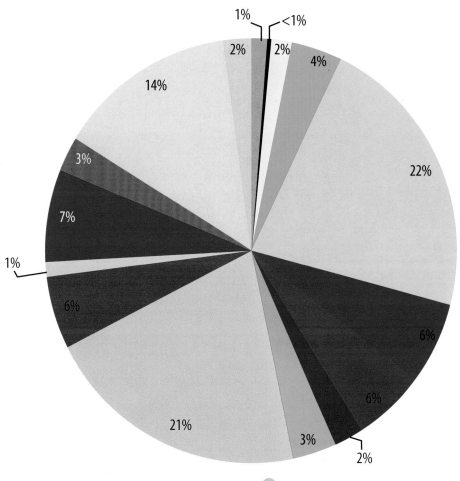

Agriculture, forestry, and fishing	$5,670	Finance, Insurance, and Real Estate	$97,376
Mining	$1,451*	Professional and Business Services	$26,053
Utilities	$7,708	Education	$5,329
Construction	$18,642	Healthcare and Social Services	$33,134
Manufacturing	$103,310	Hotels and Restaurants	$12,321
Wholesale Trade	$29,219	Government	$65,766
Retail Trade	$26,643	Other Services	$10,164
Transportation and Warehousing	$10,876	*less than 1%	
Media and Entertainment	$16,141		

Furnitureland South, near High Point, North Carolina, boasts an 85-foot-tall highboy chest of drawers, the largest piece of furniture in the world.

Goods and Services

North Carolina leads the country in the production of household furniture. High Point is nicknamed the Furniture Capital of the World. The High Point Market is the world's largest furniture trade fair.

Many of North Carolina's goods are exported to other states and countries. Chemicals are among North Carolina's most profitable exports. Factories throughout the state produce chemical products such as **pharmaceuticals**, plastics, **synthetic** fibers, and detergents.

Banks, law firms, insurance companies, hotels, restaurants, and shopping malls provide service jobs for many North Carolinians. Government employees work at public hospitals, public schools, and military bases. Some of the country's largest military bases are located in North Carolina, including Fort Bragg, Camp Lejeune Marine Corps Base, and Seymour Johnson Air Force Base.

About 29,000 students were enrolled at the University of North Carolina Chapel Hill in 2014. Among the many other state-supported schools are North Carolina State University, in Raleigh, and the University of North Carolina School of the Arts, in Winston-Salem. Duke University, located in Durham, is the largest private university in the state and one of the nation's leading universities. North Carolina also has many technical institutes and community colleges.

North Carolina is home to nearly 600 chemical and pharmaceutical companies, employing more than 61,000 people.

Fort Bragg is home to the U.S. Army Airborne Forces and Special Forces, the U.S. Army Forces Command, U.S. Army Reserve Command, and Womack Army Medical Center.

The Native American village of Pomeiooc was located near Mattamuskeet Lake in North Carolina. It was first visited and recorded by European explorers in the 1580s.

Today, Cherokee keep their culture alive through a variety of traditional crafts, including weaving.

Native Americans

Prehistoric Native Americans lived in what is now North Carolina more than 15,000 years ago. Some early Native American groups established complex societies and constructed large earthen mounds. These ceremonial mounds were built by piling many layers of dirt on top of large pits. The mounds served as places of worship and as burial sites.

Between 35,000 and 50,000 Native Americans were living in the North Carolina area when Europeans arrived in the 1500s. The Cherokee were the most numerous group when European settlements began. The Cherokee inhabited the mountains along the state's western border. Other major Native American groups included the Catawba, the Tuscarora, and the Croatans.

Native Americans in North Carolina lived primarily in settled communities. The region offered abundant resources for food, clothing, and shelter. The Native Americans grew many crops, including beans, peas, melons, pumpkins, sunflowers, and potatoes. They lived in small buildings built of wood and covered with bark.

The first European known to have explored North Carolina's coast was an Italian named Giovanni da Verrazzano. In 1524, Verrazzano wrote a report that described all of his findings. This report was sent to King Francis I of France, but the king made no attempt to colonize the region.

Timeline of Settlement

First Settlements

1584 Queen Elizabeth I of Great Britain issues a charter to Sir Walter Raleigh to begin establishing colonies in North Carolina. During the next several years, boatloads of British colonists reach Roanoke Island.

1590 After a prolonged absence, the colonial governor, John White, returns to Roanoke Island to find that the entire colony has disappeared.

1540 Hernando de Soto, a Spanish explorer, searches unsuccessfully for gold in the mountainous southwestern region.

1655 Fur trader Nathaniel Batts settles at the western end of Albemarle Sound.

1524 Giovanni da Verrazzano is the first European to explore the North Carolina coast.

Early Exploration

Colonial Development and American Revolutionary War

Spaniards were the next Europeans to explore the area. In 1540, a military expedition led by Hernando de Soto searched for gold in the mountains of southwestern North Carolina. Juan Pardo explored the same area in 1566 and 1567. Still, the Spanish made no attempt to settle the area.

Great Britain was the first European country to show interest in colonizing the North Carolina region. In 1584, Sir Walter Raleigh sent an expedition to choose a suitable site for a colony. When the explorers returned to Great Britain, they told Raleigh all about the Roanoke Island area, describing it with great enthusiasm.

Statehood and Civil War

1789 On November 21, North Carolina is the 12th state to join the Union.

1792 Raleigh is designated as North Carolina's new capital.

1776 On April 12, North Carolina becomes the first state to vote in favor of independence from Great Britain.

1861 North Carolina secedes from the Union and then sides with the Confederacy during the Civil War.

1766 New Bern becomes North Carolina's first permanent capital.

1705 Protestants from Virginia establish Bath, the first town in North Carolina.

1868 On July 4, North Carolina is readmitted to the Union as a state, three years after the Civil War ends with the Confederacy's defeat.

An annual play performed on Roanoke Island called *The Lost Colony* speculates what could have happened to Roanoke's inhabitants.

The First Settlers

In 1585, Sir Walter Raleigh sent 108 settlers to establish a colony on Roanoke Island. By 1586, food shortages and conflicts with Native Americans had forced the colonists to return to Great Britain. Eighteen men stayed behind to protect Great Britain's claim to the land. In 1587, Raleigh sent a second group of settlers to Roanoke Island. Upon their arrival in July, all that was left of the 18 men were a few skeletons.

By the end of August, the second group was running out of supplies. The governor of the colony, John White, sailed back to Great Britain for more provisions. He was forced to stay in Great Britain for three years because the country's war with Spain kept him from sailing out of British ports. When White finally returned to Roanoke Island in 1590, there was no sign of life. The entire colony had mysteriously disappeared. Today, Roanoke Island is known as the Lost Colony. The disappearance of the settlers remains a mystery.

Eventually, farmers and traders from Virginia began moving southward into North Carolina. During the 1700s, the number of colonists increased rapidly, and settlement spread westward. Much of the colony's economy was based on agriculture, and slaves worked tobacco and rice plantations. They made up a significant portion of the state's population.

In the early 1700s, the Atlantic coast was terrorized by a pirate named Edward Teach, better known as Blackbeard. In early 1718, he established a home in Bath, North Carolina, which served as a base for his piracy. Blackbeard was killed in the fall of 1718 in a battle off the coast of the Ocracoke Islands, but his legacy has made him the most famous, and notorious, pirate in the world.

Blackbeard was named because of his long black beard. He usually robbed ships off the Atlantic coast around dawn, under the cover of darkness.

From North Carolina's beginnings, tobacco was an important export. Landowners and farmers relied on slave labor to keep the lucrative industry going.

History Makers

North Carolinians have excelled in many different fields, including politics, journalism, technology, literature, and music. Three presidents have also emerged from North Carolina. Religious leaders, activists, renowned authors, and musicians have made their homes in the Tar Heel State.

Andrew Johnson (1808–1875)

Andrew Johnson grew up in North Carolina but pursued a political career in Tennessee. Although he was a southerner, he refused to support the Confederacy during the Civil War. Chosen by President Abraham Lincoln to run for vice president in 1864, Johnson became president a year later when Lincoln was shot and killed. Johnson's political opponents **impeached** him but were unable to remove him from office.

Edward R. Murrow (1908–1965)

A native of Greensboro, Edward R. Murrow was one of the most-admired radio and television journalists of the mid-twentieth century. He risked his life reporting from London while Germany was bombing Great Britain during World War II. Later, his reports for CBS News spotlighted ways in which U.S. society was not living up to its ideals.

Billy Graham (1918–)

Raised on a farm near Charlotte, Billy Graham became one of the world's best-known Protestant ministers and preachers. His Christian message has reached hundreds of millions of people through books, radio, television, newspapers, magazines, and revival meetings. Graham has met and prayed with 12 U.S. presidents.

John Coltrane (1926–1967)

John Coltrane learned to play horn and clarinet while he was growing up in High Point, and he began playing saxophone while in high school. He played with Dizzy Gillespie and Miles Davis before forming his own band. He blazed new trails for jazz in emotionally intense and harmonically daring works such as "A Love Supreme."

Maya Angelou (1928–2014)

Born in Missouri, Maya Angelou received a lifetime appointment in 1981 as professor of American Studies at Wake Forest University. Before that, she became known as a civil rights leader, poet, and nonfiction writer. Angelou's most honored work, *I Know Why the Caged Bird Sings*, describes her childhood and teenage years.

In 2009, Chapel Hill ranked number three on *Newsmax* magazine's list of "Top 25 Most Uniquely American Cities and Towns." Nearly 30,000 students enroll in Chapel Hill's University of North Carolina each year.

UNC

THE
UNIVERSITY
of
NORTH
CAROLINA
at
CHAPEL HILL

Raleigh is the second-largest city in North Carolina. As of 2014, the city was home to more than 430,000 residents.

The People Today

North Carolina is one of the nation's fastest-growing states. The population of North Carolina increased 21.4 percent between 1990 and 2000, and 18.5 percent between 2000 and 2010. Today, more than 10 million people live in the state.

The state's population is highly diverse. African Americans make up about 22 percent of the total. Many Hispanics have moved to the state, and Hispanic Americans now account for 9 percent of the population. More than 100,000 Native Americans live in North Carolina, which has one of the highest Native American populations of any state.

About 40 percent of all North Carolinians live in **rural** areas. North Carolina has one of the largest rural populations in the United States. In recent decades, the number of people living in urban areas has increased.

The Piedmont region is home to the highest concentration of people. This region contains North Carolina's largest cities. Charlotte has the largest population, followed by Raleigh, Greensboro, Winston-Salem, Durham, and Fayetteville.

Almost **3 million** more people lived in North Carolina in **2010** than in **1990**.

Q What actions do state and local governments need to take in order to keep pace with such rapid population growth?

The state capitol building in Raleigh was built in 1840. It has been named a National Historic Landmark.

State Government

North Carolina's government is divided into three branches. The legislative branch makes the state's laws. It consists of a 50-member Senate and a 120-member House of Representatives. Together, these groups of lawmakers are known as the General Assembly. All members of the General Assembly are elected to two-year terms.

The executive branch makes sure that the state's laws are carried out. The governor heads this branch and is elected to a four-year term. Other elected members of the executive branch include the lieutenant governor, secretary of state, state treasurer, and state auditor.

The judiciary is the third branch of North Carolina's government. It ensures that North Carolina's laws are obeyed. The highest court in the state is the Supreme Court. It has six associate justices and a chief justice.

After his election in 2012, Pat McCrory became the first Republican governor of North Carolina since 1993.

A statue that stands in front of North Carolina's capitol building honors presidents James Polk, Andrew Jackson, and Andrew Johnson. All three were from North Carolina.

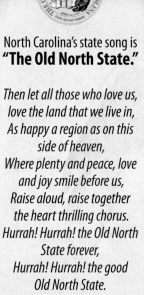

North Carolina's state song is **"The Old North State."**

Then let all those who love us,
love the land that we live in,
As happy a region as on this
side of heaven,
Where plenty and peace, love
and joy smile before us,
Raise aloud, raise together
the heart thrilling chorus.
Hurrah! Hurrah! the Old North
State forever,
Hurrah! Hurrah! the good
Old North State.

* excerpted

Reenactors help tourists envision what daily life was like for Moravians settling in Old Salem.

Celebrating Culture

The early European settlers in North Carolina represented a variety of nationalities, including British and German. Their descendants make up the majority of the state's people. German Protestants known as Moravians first immigrated to Pennsylvania before settling in North Carolina. One of the first communities established by the Moravians was Salem, which was founded in 1766 and is now known as Old Salem. A replica of the original settlement is a popular tourist site where visitors can learn about Moravian life in eighteenth-century North Carolina.

One of the largest Native American reservations in the United States is located on the western edge of North Carolina. Cherokee Native Americans share their early heritage at Oconaluftee Indian Village, which is located on the reservation. Here, visitors can watch Cherokee craftspeople demonstrate traditional arts and crafts.

African Americans have made major contributions to all aspects of life in North Carolina. African Americans honor their heritage in museums such as the African American Cultural Complex in Raleigh. In the 1950s and 1960s, African Americans in North Carolina played a pivotal role in the **civil rights movement**.

One of the most notable events happened on February 1, 1960, when four African American college students staged a sit-in at the **segregated** lunch counter in a Woolworth's store in Greensboro. The students sat at the lunch counter and were refused service, but they did not leave their seats until the restaurant closed. The next day, they returned and did the same thing. Throughout the week, more people joined the protest. The store closed its doors for a time, but in July it began serving African Americans. The sit-in served as a model for other protests against segregation throughout the South.

The Oconaluftee Indian Village is modeled after Cherokee life in the 1760s. Visitors can experience traditional Cherokee life, crafts, and food.

The Greensboro Four's sit-in was one of the most well-known examples of civil disobedience during the civil rights movement.

Actress Ava Gardner thought her character in the film *The Sun Also Rises*, Lady Brett, was one of the most interesting characters she ever played.

Arts and Entertainment

North Carolina has been home to many talented artists and performers. One of the state's best-known actors is Andy Griffith. He was raised in Mount Airy and starred in many popular television series, including *The Andy Griffith Show*. Born in Grabtown in 1922, Ava Gardner starred in numerous Hollywood films, including *Show Boat* and *The Sun Also Rises*.

Many gifted visual artists come from North Carolina. Bob Timberlake, a native of Lexington, is known for his beautifully detailed paintings. His work can be seen in museums across the country. The North Carolina Museum of Art, located in Raleigh, features an artwork collection ranging from ancient Egyptian pieces to contemporary works.

The **North Carolina Symphony**, founded in 1943, was one of the first state symphonies in the United States.

The **North Carolina Museum of Art** was the first state-funded art museum in the country.

North Carolina has a strong literary tradition. Novelist and playwright Thomas Wolfe was born in Asheville in 1900. Short-story writer William Sydney Porter, who wrote under the **pen name** O. Henry, was born in Greensboro in 1862. His stories, widely read in the twentieth century, were known for their surprise endings.

Unveiled in 1985, O. Henry's Book has become a popular monument in Greensboro. The bronze statue depicts two of O. Henry's stories, "The Gift of the Magi" and "The Ransom of Red Chief."

Many celebrated musicians have hailed from North Carolina. John Coltrane ranks as one of the greatest saxophone players, composers, and bandleaders in jazz history. Other musicians who were born or raised in the state include Nina Simone, Roberta Flack, James Taylor, Ryan Adams, and Ronnie Milsap.

Nina Simone was a gifted pianist, singer, songwriter, author, and civil rights activist.

Sports and Recreation

North Carolina's mountains and seacoast offer excellent recreational opportunities. The state's four national forests and dozens of state parks feature hiking and mountain biking trails and other outdoor challenges. Rock climbers scale the vertical cliffs at Hanging Rock State Park, while hang gliders soar over massive sand dunes at Jockey's Ridge State Park.

The state's coastal areas are havens for those who enjoy sea kayaking, windsurfing, scuba diving, and other water sports. Long stretches of unspoiled beaches along the Outer Banks are also popular spots for sunbathing and swimming. Many rivers in the state offer excellent opportunities for whitewater rafting, and the scenic lakes are ideal for canoeing.

Mia Hamm, who played soccer at the University of North Carolina, helped lead the U.S. women's team to a **gold medal** at the 2004 **Summer Olympic Games.**

Stock-car racing is very popular in North Carolina, and the leading track is the **Charlotte Motor Speedway**.

Hanging Rock State Park boasts more than 20 miles of hiking trails, many of which lead to spectacular views of the park.

Many famous athletes have been associated with North Carolina. World-renowned boxer Sugar Ray Leonard was born in Rocky Mount and raised in Wilmington. During his impressive boxing career, he won several world titles and an Olympic gold medal. Dale Earnhardt Sr., born in Kannapolis, was one of the most dominant **NASCAR** drivers of the 1980s and 1990s. His son, Dale Earnhardt Jr., has also won a wide following among NASCAR fans.

Cam Newton became quarterback for the Charlotte Panthers in 2011. In 2016, he made his first Super Bowl appearance with the team.

College basketball is one of the most popular team sports in the state. North Carolina is home to four college basketball teams in the Atlantic Coast Conference. They are the University of North Carolina Tar Heels, the Duke Blue Devils, the North Carolina State University Wolfpack, and the Wake Forest University Demon Deacons. Among the state's professional teams are the Charlotte Hornets of the National Basketball Association, the Carolina Panthers of the National Football League, and the Carolina Hurricanes of the National Hockey League.

Two-time Daytona 500 winner Dale Earnhardt Jr. is one of the most recognizable names in NASCAR history.

Get To Know NORTH CAROLINA

The first **miniature golf course** in the U.S. was built in Fayetteville, North Carolina, in 1913.

NORTH CAROLINA HAS **150** RADIO STATIONS AND MORE THAN **30** TELEVISION STATIONS.

The **largest** alligator found in North Carolina was **12 feet, 7 inches** from **head** to **tail.**

The world's first **Krispy Kreme** donut shop opened in Winston-Salem in 1937.

PEPSI WAS INVENTED IN NEW BERN, NORTH CAROLINA, IN 1898.

The largest emerald found in North America, at 1,438 carats, was discovered in North Carolina in 1969.

The Cape Hatteras Lighthouse is the **tallest lighthouse** in the U.S.

What have you learned about North Carolina after reading this book? Test your knowledge by answering these questions. All of the information can be found in the text you just read. The answers are provided below for easy reference.

1 What three natural land regions make up North Carolina?

2 What is the main crop grown in North Carolina?

3 In what year did Sir Walter Raleigh establish a colony on Roanoke Island?

4 Where did the pirate Blackbeard have his final battle in 1718?

5 What is the name of North Carolina's National Football League team?

6 About how many Native Americans live in North Carolina today?

7 Which restaurant did four African American college students stage a protest in by sitting at the counter?

8 What city in North Carolina is known as the "Furniture Capital of the World"?

ANSWER KEY
1. The Piedmont, the Atlantic Coastal Plain, and the Appalachian Mountains
2. Tobacco 3. 1585 4. The Ocracoke Islands 5. Carolina Panthers
6. 100,000 7. Woolworth's 8. High Point

Key Words

abolished: ended

alluvial: deposits of clay or sand left behind by flowing water

archaeologists: scientists who study early peoples through artifacts and remains

carnivorous: flesh-eating

civil rights movement: the struggle to achieve racial equality for African Americans

impeached: formally charged with wrongdoing

NASCAR: National Association for Stock Car Auto Racing

pen name: an assumed name used by a writer

pharmaceuticals: drugs and medicines

reservoirs: places where water is collected and stored

rural: relating to the countryside

segregated: racially separated and restricted

synthetic: artificially made

Index

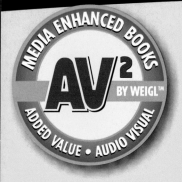

Log on to www.av2books.com

AV[2] by Weigl brings you media enhanced books that support active learning. Go to www.av2books.com, and enter the special code found on page 2 of this book. You will gain access to enriched and enhanced content that supplements and complements this book. Content includes video, audio, weblinks, quizzes, a slide show, and activities.

AV[2] Online Navigation

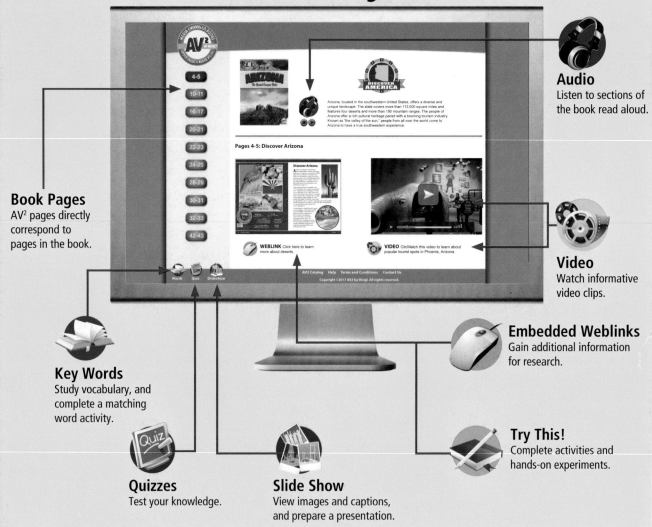

Book Pages
AV[2] pages directly correspond to pages in the book.

Audio
Listen to sections of the book read aloud.

Video
Watch informative video clips.

Embedded Weblinks
Gain additional information for research.

Key Words
Study vocabulary, and complete a matching word activity.

Try This!
Complete activities and hands-on experiments.

Quizzes
Test your knowledge.

Slide Show
View images and captions, and prepare a presentation.

AV[2] was built to bridge the gap between print and digital. We encourage you to tell us what you like and what you want to see in the future.

Sign up to be an AV[2] Ambassador at www.av2books.com/ambassador.

Due to the dynamic nature of the Internet, some of the URLs and activities provided as part of AV[2] by Weigl may have changed or ceased to exist. AV[2] by Weigl accepts no responsibility for any such changes. All media enhanced books are regularly monitored to update addresses and sites in a timely manner. Contact AV[2] by Weigl at 1-866-649-3445 or av2books@weigl.com with any questions, comments, or feedback.